T0013940

Differences Matter
DIVERSITY MATTERS

A Story About My Brother and Me

Justin Blount

ILLUSTRATED BY
Wendi Hendra Saputra

Young Authors Publishing

Young Authors Publishing
www.youngauthorspublishing.org

Book Design by April Mostek

Our books may be purchased in bulk
for promotional, educational, or business use.
Please contact Young Authors Publishing by email at
info@youngauthorspublishing.org.

Dedication

I would like to dedicate my book to my baby brother Noah. Noah and I have different physical attributes. Everyone is unique, which makes the world more enjoyable. Due to our differences, he has taught me how to have a voice. Through his teachings, I truly embrace the ideas of self-love and knowledge.

Racial and cultural diversity is important because it allows for freedom and awareness. It also brings people together to show us how our history has evolved.

Most importantly, it shows us that everybody has a purpose and that social awareness breaks down social and racial barriers.

I am a young African American activist named Justin who attends the public school system and I strongly believe in racial equality. As a student in the public school system, I have always felt that the American education system has never provided a full multicultural contribution to their curriculum.

All I can think about is how I can attend a school where children from every race, every background, and every community can come together, and become brothers and sisters, to accomplish a certain goal.

My father taught my brother and I to always treat people with compassion and kindness, how to keep a balance, and keep things in perspective. Lastly, he taught me to advocate! And with great opportunity, I will always advocate for cultural diversity and inclusion.

I am a part of a family that is multicultural and multiracial. My little brother Noah and I are like peanut butter and jelly. I am Black and Noah is White, but we are most definitely still two peas in a pod! For this reason, I want to create an opportunity to engage in more conversations on students being culturally aware.

Over the weekend, my little brother Noah and I went to my cousin Brody's birthday party. We were all playing football and having fun when Brody's friends started making fun of Noah because of his gender and the color of his skin.

When we left the party, I remained quiet the whole ride home. My father knew that I was upset about something, so he sat me down and had a conversation with me. I informed my father of what happened with Brody and his friends.

My father told me, "Everyone is different, and people are confused because they don't understand that people have similarities, but differences also. The two of you are brothers, even if you are from two different backgrounds. Most of your peers will not be culturally aware, and it is okay that people have multiracial family members. You will always be a trendsetter, who's going to break down social and racial barriers. You will be a part of the solution and part of the change."

The next morning, I was still feeling a little down about what happened at the party. While at lunch, one of my peers made another comment about my brother's differences. He made me feel a little uneasy because I was still upset from what happened over the weekend.

I had enough! Something needed to be done! I decided to create an initiative for a cultural and inclusion task force. I needed an explanation, but most importantly I wanted to make sure my peers became more socially and culturally aware.

When lunch was over, I went to visit my school counselors Ms. Blaire and Dr. Monroe to tell them what happened over the weekend and what just happened at lunch.

Once I was finished, I informed them that I wanted to start a Multicultural Awareness Day at our middle school. They were very excited to see my enthusiasm for cultural diversity and inclusion and said they would love to help.

I was very excited and went to class to tell my favorite math teacher Ms. Farrah-Phillips about Multicultural Awareness Day. Ms. Farrah-Phillips wanted to know how this came about and I told her what happened at lunch and over the weekend.

She was surprised to hear what happened and asked me if I felt comfortable sharing my experiences with my classmates. I said "yes" as they all filed in the classroom after recess.

Once everyone was seated, I looked at Ms. Farrah-Phillips and she gave me the okay to start. I began to share my family's story with my classmates. I was excited because I knew this was the only way they would become more aware and receive more knowledge.

After I was finished, some of my friends raised their hands and asked questions. I answered them the best way I could, then Ms. Farrah-Phillips gave me a pass to see Principal Farin-Hampton.

Once I got to the principal's office, I sat down with Principal Farin-Hampton and asked her if we could have a Multicultural Awareness Day at our middle school.

Principal Farin-Hampton asked, "Justin, why do you feel it is important to have a Multicultural Awareness Day at school?" I replied, "Because, it is important to support children across all racial groups and ethnicities, especially in a school setting. It makes everyone feel important, loved, and included."

Principal Farin-Hampton said, "Well then, I'll support it! What would this day include? What would this day look like?" I thought about this a little and said, "Students can wear their traditional clothing to represent their culture, bring their food from their culture, and the whole school can engage in a multicultural dance in the cafeteria!"

Principal Farin-Hampton gave me the okay and said we could have the multicultural celebration as soon as next week! I was really excited to plan the Multicultural Awareness Day. We created a committee right on the spot and Principal Farin-Hampton prepared an email to get everyone prepped and ready, starting tomorrow.

It had been a long, but truly rewarding week. I was really excited that my principal accepted and supported my idea for a Multicultural Awareness Day! This made me feel really good because my teacher, my counselors, and my classmates all supported my idea. This made me really happy.

Principal Farin-Hampton said that this could be an ongoing celebration every year at our middle school. I now feel that we are all working as a team to bring cultural awareness and diversity inclusion to our school.

What Can Readers Do?

In school and even outside of school, children should learn to appreciate all differences. Parents should answer children's questions about differences honestly and respectfully. For example:

1. **EDUCATE:** Parents and teachers can educate children on the many different cultures in the world. Doing this will help bring awareness to holidays that different cultures have and how they celebrate them.

2. **LANGUAGE:** Teach children different words in the native languages that are spoken in their classroom community.

3. **BOOKS:** Choose different kinds of children's books to educate children on different races, different family cultures and dynamics, and most importantly, books that will help them understand their identity.

4. **LIFE EXPERIENCES:** Parents and teachers can encourage friendships in their classrooms with different races and ethnically diverse peers and classmates. With these life experiences, they can expose children to different foods from different cultures and different clothing.

5. **EVENTS:** Parents should encourage their children to attend different cultural events and celebrations.

6. **FILMS:** Parents can encourage their children to watch age appropriate films about other cultures.

About the Author

Justin Blount is an 11-year-old activist from Atlanta, Georgia. At a young age, Justin saw the need for bringing awareness to racial equality and began advocating for diversity and inclusion in his community. In addition to advocacy, Justin loves music because he believes that music has a way of bringing people of different cultures and nationalities together. When Justin grows up, he wants to have a career as a music instructor.

ABOUT YOUNG AUTHORS PUBLISHING

We believe that all kids are story-worthy!

Young Authors Publishing is a children's book publisher that exists to share the diverse stories of Black and Brown children.

How We're Different

Young Authors participate in a 1-month 'Experience Program' where they are paired with a trained writing mentor that helps them conceptualize and write their very own children's book. Once their manuscript is completed, our young authors attend workshops to learn the fundamentals of financial literacy, entrepreneurship, and public speaking in an effort to ensure they have the tools they need to succeed as successful published writers. Young Authors Publishing is on a mission to empower the authors of tomorrow, using their words to change the dialogue around representation in literature.

Learn more about our impact at
www.youngauthorspublishing.org

YOUNG
AUTHORS
PUBLISHING